SPRING CREEK MEDIA CENTER
6001 S. 3rd St.
Broken Arrow, OK 74

Happy St. Patrick's Day

Author: Mercer, Abbie.
Reading Level: 3.5 LG
Point Value: 0.5
ACCELERATED READER QUIZ 117328

Happy ST. PATRICK'S DAY

Holiday Fun

ABBIE MERCER

PowerKiDS press
New York

For my mother, in thanks for Mr. Kilpatrick

Published in 2008 by The Rosen Publishing Group, Inc.
29 East 21st Street, New York, NY 10010

Copyright © 2008 by The Rosen Publishing Group, Inc.

All rights reserved. No part of this book may be reproduced in any form without permission in writing from the publisher, except by a reviewer.

First Edition

Editor: Amelie von Zumbusch
Book Design: Julio Gil
Photo Researcher: Nicole Pristash

Photo Credits: Cover, pp. 1, 5, 7, 9, 15, 17, 19 © Getty Images; pp. 11, 11 (inset), 13, 21, 21 (inset) © Shutterstock.com; p. 13 (inset) © www.istockphoto.com/Rick Rhay.

Library of Congress Cataloging-in-Publication Data

Mercer, Abbie.
　Happy St. Patrick's Day / Abbie Mercer. — 1st ed.
　　　p. cm. — (Holiday fun)
　Includes bibliographical references and index.
　ISBN-13: 978-1-4042-3811-4 (library binding : alk. paper)
　ISBN-10: 1-4042-3811-5 (library binding : alk. paper)
　1. Saint Patrick's Day—Juvenile literature. I. Title.
　GT4995.P3M47 2008
　394.262—dc22

2007004034

Manufactured in the United States of America

Contents

What Is St. Patrick's Day?	4
Who Was St. Patrick?	6
St. Patrick and the Irish	8
Symbols of St. Patrick's Day	10
How to Plant Shamrocks	12
Leprechauns and Banshees	14
Parades	16
Irish Dancing	18
How to Cook Irish Soda Bread	20
Celebrating St. Patrick's Day	22
Glossary	23
Index	24
Web Sites	24

What Is St. Patrick's Day?

St. Patrick's Day is a special holiday that comes each year on March 17. It is a day for Irish people to **celebrate** their country. Many Americans and Canadians whose family came from Ireland honor their family's homeland on this day. People whose family is not Irish can celebrate St. Patrick's Day, too. It is a great time to have a party and learn about the **traditions** of another land.

Some people tell Irish stories and sing Irish songs on St. Patrick's Day. Others honor this holiday by marching in a parade or going to a party.

These girls are taking part in a St. Patrick's Day parade in Philadelphia, Pennsylvania.

Who Was St. Patrick?

St. Patrick's Day honors a **Christian** saint, or holy person, named St. Patrick. St. Patrick was born in Britain in the late 300s. When he was about 16, Patrick was carried off to Ireland and sold into **slavery**. After six years of slavery in Ireland, Patrick had a dream. He believed that he heard the voice of God telling him to leave Ireland. Patrick ran away from Ireland and became a **priest**.

Although he had suffered in Ireland, Patrick decided to return there after becoming a priest. He hoped to help the Irish people and to get them to become Christians.

When St. Patrick came to Ireland as a priest, he got hundreds of people to become Christians.

St. Patrick and the Irish

In Ireland, St. Patrick caused many people to become Christians and founded many churches. Some people even claim he drove all the snakes out of Ireland! In time, St. Patrick became one of the **patron saints** of Ireland. The Irish people honored St. Patrick's Day by going to church, feasting, and dancing.

In the 1840s, crops failed all over Ireland. People did not have enough food to eat. Many people died. Others moved to the United States, hoping to find a better life. The Irish kept celebrating St. Patrick's Day in the United States because it helped them remember their homeland.

When their crops failed, many Irish families had no food. This time is often called the Great Hunger.

Symbols of St. Patrick's Day

Over time, St. Patrick's Day became a celebration of Ireland, as well as of St. Patrick. Many of the **symbols** of Ireland became symbols of St. Patrick's Day. For example, people often wear green on St. Patrick's Day because green is a symbol of Ireland. This is because Ireland gets lots of light rain, which causes many leafy, green plants to grow there.

Ireland's best-known green plant is the shamrock. Shamrocks are small plants with three leaves on every stem. They grow wild in Ireland and many other parts of the world. Shamrocks are another symbol of St. Patrick's Day.

Ireland is well known for its green countryside. Inset: Each of a shamrock's three leaves is heart shaped.

How to Plant Shamrocks

Shamrocks grow outside or inside. It is easy to plant a pot of shamrocks to brighten up your house.

1 Fill a flowerpot three-quarters of the way up with dirt, like the girl on page 13. You can use dirt from your garden or buy dirt called potting soil.

2 Buy a pack of shamrock seeds. Sprinkle, or loosely drop, the seeds over the dirt in your flowerpot. Then sprinkle enough dirt over the seeds to cover them fully.

3 Water your seeds. Check the pot each day to see if the seeds need more water. The soil should always be dark and a little wet.

4 When the shamrock plants sprout, or appear, put the pot in a sunny place. Make sure to keep watering it. Soon you will have lots of green shamrock leaves, like the plant on page 13.

Leprechauns and Banshees

Like shamrocks, leprechauns are symbols of St. Patrick's Day. Irish stories say that a leprechaun is a **fairy** man who makes shoes for other fairies. The fairies pay a leprechaun in gold. Leprechauns always hide their gold, but if you catch a leprechaun, he will tell you where his gold is hidden.

Leprechauns are just one of the many kinds of fairies that appear in traditional Irish stories. Another kind of fairy is the banshee. Banshees are fairy women who are tied to a human family. When a member of that family dies, you can hear the banshee **keening**.

This man is dressed up as a leprechaun in honor of St. Patrick's Day.

Parades

While some people tell old Irish stories to celebrate St. Patrick's Day, others watch or march in a parade. Strangely enough, the very first St. Patrick's Day parade took place in the United States rather than Ireland. In 1762, Irishmen serving in the British army held a St. Patrick's Day parade in New York City.

Today, New York City still holds a big parade. Other cities, such as Chicago, Illinois, and Boston, Massachusetts, have important parades, too. Many of these parades have **floats** and marching bands. Police officers, Irish groups, and dancers also take part in many parades.

These men are playing music on bagpipes in a St. Patrick's Day parade in Chicago, Illinois.

Irish Dancing

Irish dancers take part in many St. Patrick's Day parades. These dancers do a type of traditional Irish dancing called step dancing. Step dancers move their feet very quickly and exactly. They do not move their arms or upper body at all. Many step dancers are young boys and girls. Most dancers are trained in special step-dancing schools.

There are two kinds of Irish step dancing, soft shoe and hard shoe. Hard-shoe dancers wear heavy shoes to beat out loud **rhythms**. Soft-shoe dancers wear soft, quiet shoes. The reel and the light jig are well-known soft-shoe dances.

Girls often wear special dresses with colorful patterns when they do Irish dancing.

How to Cook Irish Soda Bread

Eating traditional Irish foods is another way to celebrate St. Patrick's Day. One of the best-liked Irish foods is Irish soda bread. Ask an adult for help when using the oven or a knife.

Turn the oven on to 375° F (190° C). Then mix 3 cups (460 g) flour, 1 teaspoon salt, and 1 teaspoon baking soda in a large bowl. Add 1¼ cups (300 ml) buttermilk to the bowl. Mix it all together until the flour drinks in the buttermilk. Start mixing with a spoon, but then use your hands, like the girl on page 21.

Spread a little bit of flour on a clean tabletop. Put the bread dough, or batter, on top of the flour. Rub the dough together until it forms one ball.

Shape the bread into a circle and put it on a cookie sheet. Carefully use a knife to cut a big *X* across the top of the bread.

Bake the bread for about 45 minutes. Then take it out of the oven and let it cool for 10 minutes. It should look like the bread on page 21. The bread is best if you eat it while it is still a little bit warm.

Celebrating St. Patrick's Day

Irish soda bread is not the only Irish food people eat on St. Patrick's Day. Some people eat a thick soup called Irish stew. Others sip drinks that were dyed green for St. Patrick's Day. To make a green drink, add a few drops of green food coloring to a glass of milk.

Lots of people say "Everyone is Irish on St. Patrick's Day." This means you need not really be Irish to celebrate St. Patrick's Day. The Irish happily share their celebration and traditions with people from around the world. Next March 17, remember to wear green and have fun!

Glossary

celebrate (SEH-luh-brayt) To honor an important moment by doing special things.

Christian (KRIS-chun) Having to do with someone who follows the teachings of Jesus Christ and the Bible.

fairy (FER-ee) A being with magical powers.

floats (FLOHTS) Low, flat trucks that carry people and sets in a parade.

keening (KEEN-ing) Crying in a loud, high way.

patron saints (PAY-trun SAYNTS) Holy people who are tied to a place or group of people.

priest (PREEST) A person who is trained to act for God in a church service.

rhythms (RIH-thumz) Movements with a rise and fall.

slavery (SLAY-vuh-ree) The system of one person "owning" another.

symbols (SIM-bulz) Objects or pictures that stand for something else.

traditions (truh-DIH-shunz) Ways of doing something that have been passed down over time.

Index

A
Americans, 4

B
Britain, 6

C
Canadians, 4

D
dream, 6

F
family, 4, 14
floats, 16

H
homeland, 4, 8

I
Ireland, 4, 6, 8, 10, 16
Irish people, 4, 6, 8
Irish songs, 4
Irish stories, 4, 14, 16

M
March 17, 4, 22

P
parade(s), 4, 16, 18
party, 4

patron saints, 8
priest, 6

R
rhythms, 18

S
slavery, 6
symbols, 10, 14

T
traditions, 4, 22

V
voice, 6

Web Sites

Due to the changing nature of Internet links, PowerKids Press has developed an online list of Web sites related to the subject of this book. This site is updated regularly. Please use this link to access the list:
www.powerkidslinks.com/hfun/pat/